M000311528

A little Book for Grandfather

A Little Book for Grandfather

Patrick Regan

Andrews McMeel
Publishing, LLC

Kansas City

07 08 09 10 11 TEP 10 9 8 7 6 5 4 3 2 1

ISBN-13: 978-0-7407-6406-6
ISBN-10: 0-7407-6406-3

Library of Congress Control Number: 2006933028

www.andrewsmcmeel.com

Introduction

Few things are more delightful than grandchildren fighting over your lap.

–Doug Larson

There is nothing quite like the bond between a grandfather and his grandchild. Separated by a generation, each regards the other with a certain fascination. The grandchild is intrigued and amazed by the span of experiences and the different world the grandfather has known. The grandfather sees in his grandchild nothing less than a glimpse of the future.

For grandchildren, grandpas are endlessly enjoyable. They are a bottomless source of stories set in days long gone by, of curious whistled tunes, early morning fishing trips, and sleight-of-hand magic tricks. Whether answering a barrage of questions about life when he was a kid or folding an especially tricky paper airplane, no one is more patient. When it comes to his grandkids, a grandpa seems to have all the time in the world.

Of course, the relationship pays off both ways. A grandfather gets to see young eyes light up at his arrival. He gets to feel that delightful weight of a toddler on his knee. And he gets a rapt audience for those stories he loves to tell. He gets a second chance to play. A grandfather and a grandchild each invites the other into a world neither could know without the other. Now, what could be more grand than that?

Grandchildren don't stay young forever, which is good because Pop-pops have only so many horsey rides in them.

Gene Perret

Being grandparents sufficiently removes us from the responsibilities so that we can be friends.

Allan Frome

One of the most powerful handclasps is that of a new grandbaby around the finger of a grandfather.

Joy Hargrove

A grandparent is old on the outside but young on the inside.

Anonymous

A child needs a grandparent, anybody's grandparent, to grow a little more securely into an unfamiliar world.

Charles and Ann Morse

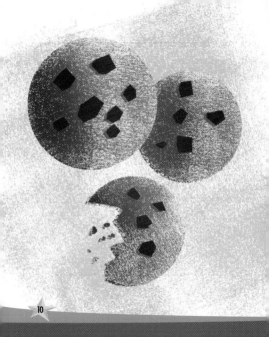

What children need most are the essentials that grandparents provide in abundance. They give unconditional love, kindness, patience, humor, comfort, lessons in life. And, most importantly, cookies.

Rudolph Giuliani

The best place to be when you're sad is Grandpa's lap.

Anonymous

The best thing
grandfathers
can give their
grandchildren
is time.

Willard Scott

The generations of living things pass in a short time, and like runners hand on the torch of life.

Lucretius

It's funny what
happens when
you become a
grandparent.
You start to act
all goofy and do
things you never
thought you'd do.
It's terrific.

Mike Krzyzewski

There are fathers who
do not love their children;
there is no grandfather
who does not adore
his grandson.

Victor Hugo

Grandchildren don't make a man feel old; it's the knowledge that he's married to a grandmother.

G. Norman Collie

Perfect love
sometimes does
not come until the
first grandchild.

Welsh proverb

My grandpa didn't believe in hugging and kissing, or saying "I love you." His love had to do with the way he treated you. When he said, "We're going here, we're going there," he was telling me about life. That was his love for me. My love for him was listening to what he said, keeping out of trouble, doing right, being fair.

Bill Cosby

Whoever teaches his son teaches not alone his son but also his son's son, and so on to the end of generations.

Hebrew proverb

It's amazing how grandparents seem so young once you become one.

Anonymous

Remember the days of old, consider the years of many generations: ask thy father, and he will show thee; thy elders, and they will tell thee.

King James Bible, Deuteronomy 32:7

Nobody can do for little children what grandparents do. Grandparents sort of sprinkle stardust over the lives of little children.

Alex Haley

Every generation revolts against its fathers and makes friends with its grandfathers.

Lewis Mumford

I have a warm feeling after playing with my grandchildren. It's the liniment working.

Anonymous

The simplest toy, one which even the youngest child can operate, is called a grandparent.

Sam Levenson

In order to influence
a child, one must
be careful not to be
that child's parent or
grandparent.

Don Marquis

The best babysitters, of course, are the baby's grandparents. You feel completely comfortable entrusting your baby to them for long periods, which is why most grandparents flee to Florida.

Dave Barry

If you look deeply into the palm of your hand, you will see your parents and all generations of your ancestors. All of them are alive in this moment. Each is present in your body. You are the continuation of each of these people.

Thich Nhat Hanh

44

Posterity is the patriotic name for grandchildren.

Art Linkletter

What a bargain
grandchildren are!
I give them my
loose change, and
they give me a
million dollars'
worth of pleasure.

Gene Perret

You've got to do
your own growing,
no matter how tall
your grandfather was.

Irish proverb

They say genes
skip generations.
Maybe that's why
grandparents find
their grandchildren
so likable.

Joan McIntosh

Grandparents,
like heroes, are as
necessary to a child's
growth as vitamins.

Joyce Allston

One of life's greatest mysteries is how the boy who wasn't good enough to marry your daughter can be the father of the smartest grandchild in the world.

Anonymous

If you want to know where I come by the passionate commitment I have to bringing people together without regard to race, it all started with my grandfather.

Bill Clinton

Elephants and grandchildren never forget.

Andy Rooney

My grandfather was a wonderful role model. Through him I got to know the gentle side of men.

Sarah Long

Our grandchildren accept us for ourselves, without rebuke or effort to change us, as no one in our entire lives has ever done, not our parents, siblings, spouses, friends—and hardly ever our own grown children.

Ruth Goode

The older generation thought nothing of getting up at five every morning— and the younger generation doesn't think much of it either.

John J. Welsh

Our children are here to stay, but our babies and toddlers and preschoolers are gone as fast as they can grow up—and we have only a short moment with each. When you see a grandfather take a baby in his arms, you see that the moment hasn't always been long enough.

St. Clair Adams Sullivan

My grandfather once told me that there are two kinds of people: those who work and those who take the credit. He told me to try to be in the first group; there was less competition there.

Indira Gandhi

In every conceivable manner, the family is link to our past, bridge to our future.

Alex Haley

**No cowboy
was ever faster
on the draw than
a grandparent
pulling a baby
picture out of
a wallet.**

Anonymous

What is it about grandparents that is so lovely? I'd like to say that grandparents are God's gifts to children. And if they can but see, hear, and feel what these people have to give, they can mature at a fast rate.

Bill Cosby